Capp Road

Matt Borczon

Nixes Mate Books
Allston, Massachusetts

Copyright © 2017 Matt Borczon

Book design by d'Entremont
Cover photographs by Jay Miner

All rights reserved. This book or any portion thereof may not be reproduced or used in any manner whatsoever without the express written permission of the publisher except for the use of brief quotations in a book review or scholarly journal.

Some of these poems appeared in *Pressure Press*, *the Beatnik Cowboy*, *Stay Weird and keep writing*, and *Horror Trash Sleeze*.

Thanks and love to Dana, Hannah, Ezra Jonah and Eliza for being the reason I want to tell my story.

ISBN 978-0-9991882-4-8

Nixes Mate Books
POBox 1179
Allston, MA 02134
nixesmate.pub/books

To Dr. Seward who taught my poetry writing class in Edinboro. He once read a poem I wrote and asked me why my description of Edinboro, PA was so harsh.

Contents

demographics	1
Rick	4
Gabe	6
Capp Rd.	8
Debie	10
Laura	12
Randy	14
Baling hay	16
Buffalo	18
Gabe 2	20
Action movie	23
Cutter	24
Chris	26
Psycho	28

Gabe 3	30
Gunga Dan	32
good on paper	35
Caretaking	37
Debie 2	40
Billy	41
Brian	43
The Hokker Brothers	46
Sara	48
Debbie's goodbye note	50
Tim	52
Wanda	54
personal history	56

Capp Road

demographics

it's a
college town
with a
fake lake
surrounded
by dairy farms

it's skinny kids
who will
need college
to get
jobs to
save land
their families
owned for
generations

its home
to one
of the
first recorded
school shootings
in America

an 8th grade
student shoots

a teacher
through
the head
at the
graduation dance
while kids were
close dancing
to the
theme from
Titanic

the air
is full of
diesel smoke
and brown
dust from
dirt roads
the smell
of manure
blue misery
and secrets
kept inside
of dark trailers

its functional
alcoholism
and codependence

it's a place
to want
to leave.

Rick

Rick was
new to
the family
had been
with Jenny
only a
few months
so when
the kids
wanted to
keep the
litter of
kittens born
to their
barn cat
he was
happy to
say yes.

After the
first one
got sick
they begged
him to
take them
all to

the vet
but he
told them
to go
play outside.

They both
heard the
gun shots
and Kim
told me
later that
she never
forgot the
look on
Rick's face
that night
as he
sat there
downing shots
of whiskey
trying not
to cry
the pistol
still in
his lap.

Gabe

as a
kid Gabe
took out
a friends
eye with
a stick
sword fighting

as a
teen ager
he thought
he'd join
the priesthood
practiced the
2 handed
hand shake
and the
too wide
smile

By college
he had
started following
girls home
at night
Gabe swore

he could
hear them
call to
him from
their dorm
rooms miles
away said
he knew
which ones
were in
love with
him

he told
me that
the first
one who
had him
arrested
was using
an overdue
library book
to taunt
his soul.

Capp Rd.

is full
of shit
smelling
cow farms
and there
are dead
animals
everywhere
because the
kids drive
the dirt
roads like
there's no
tomorrow

maybe its
because their
closest
neighbors
are miles
away or
maybe it's
to create
the illusion
that their
lives are

going
farther than
the local
university

that their
lives are
going
anywhere

other than
here.

Debie

everyone
thought she
would end
up with
Eddie
but even
she called
him old
farmer Ed
and she
laughed at
the train
conductors hat
he wore

when ever
we would
walk up
Capp road
if there
was a
dead animal
she'd punch
me in
the arm
and yell

hold your
breath
and run

so death
can't get
inside.

Laura

grew up
in a
trailer
on a
farm her
daddy worked

she joined
the Army
and learned
Russian
worked as
a code
breaker
before coming
home to
attend the
local college

she loved
to tell
me that
the problem
with the
men in
this town

is that
there are
no men
in this
town

Randy

had
long stringy
black hair
and wore
a full
length
fur coat
even in
summer
they say
he raises
pit bulls
they say
he's a
bad ass
spent time
in prison
but one
night at
the wayside
tavern
big Jeff
tells him
he's full
of shit
and when

Randy says
sounds like
somebody wants
to rumble
Jeff just
laughs and
puts his
9mm on
the bar

Randy was
gone before
Jeff could
take off
his wedding
ring.

Baling hay

Ed's dad
had a
masters degree
and drove
the local
school bus
all to
help keep
the families
dairy farm
up on
it's wheels

he used
to hire
all of
Ed's friends
to bale
hay in
summer
it was
hot sticky
and the
hay was
heavier

than it
looked

after my
first day
he said
you work
pretty hard
for a
city boy.

Buffalo

lives
in a
trailer that
looks
abandoned
from the
outside
they say
his dad
lost the
farm and
his little
half acre
is all
that's left

we all
go there
to buy
weed
Buffalo is
over 300
pounds and
keeps a
sawed off
shot gun

behind
his door
says he
has no
future plans
except
to keep
farming
until he
dies.

Gabe 2

he took
me to
court over
money for
kung fu
class but
lost
then he
wrote a
40 page
letter to
my instructor
outlining
his superiority
which was
supposed
to be the
reason
I would
not promote
him

when I
saw him
I offered
to fight

him for
the belt
he wanted
but he
ran off

a year
later
he was
back
in town
telling
everyone
he knows
how to
pronounce
my demon
name and
that is
why I
am so
threatened
by him
he makes
a gut wrenching

noise to
demonstrate

Gabe says
I can't
kill him
because
he has
no blood
that his
 body is
completely
full of
ether.

Action movie

We're sitting
in the
local
movie house
watching an
action flick
when a
guy gets
killed by
being thrown
into a
giant farm
machine
farmer Ed
leans over
and says
I have
never seen
any machine
like that
on any
farm
anywhere
ever.

Cutter

there were
so many
bullet holes
in her
street sign
you couldn't
read it

her step
dad poached
deer to
feed the
family in
winter

her dog
had only
one eye
and her
brother was
dishonorably
discharged from
the army

I never
noticed

where she
cut herself
until after
I found
the bottle
full of
blood under
the couch

I'm still
not sure
why
I was
surprised.

Chris

right after
boot camp
he tattooed
the first
article of
the code
of conduct
in bold
black letters
around his
wrist.

this was
before he
deployed
before he
found out
if he
really was
prepared
to give
his life
for his
country.
Now most
nights he

sits in
the back
booth with
his back
pressed up
on the
wall nursing
a gin
and tonic
and using
a penny
to try
to scratch
that tattoo
out of
his skin.

Psycho

was covered
in tattoos
neck face
hands all
over and
he wore
a bandana
while he
delivered
pizza to
nervous coeds
and drunken
frat boys
on his
motorcycle

most everyone
was scared
of him but
his friends
told me
that he
wasn't always
like this
after
the graduation

dance where
we all saw
our teacher
killed…
man
it changed
all of us
but him
most of
all.

Gabe 3

I didn't
know what
schizophrenia
was back
then and
I don't
think Gabe
knew either
but we
think he
must have
had it

right up
until the
night he
followed
a girl
into NY
state
he was
sure she
was in
love with
him and
her father

shot him
3 times
in the
chest as
he tried
to convince
her.

Gunga Dan

owned a
pair of
Chuck Norris
kicking jeans
and wore
razor blades
taped into
his collar
just
in case

he and
Chris joined
the navy
right out
of high
school
a couple
years later
Dan stepped
on an
IED in Iraq
losing his
left arm
both legs
and his

junk as
well

he says
they took
a sperm
sample
on the
operating
table in
case he
meets a
girl who
wants kids
but we
doubt this
will ever
happen
because
Dan spends
all day
smoking weed
and watching
action movies

sitting

in his
wheel chair
he talks
about how
things should
have been
different.

good on paper

we booked
a church
bought a
dress and
told our
families
only we
never mentioned
the part
where we
no longer
got along
Debbie
was good
at making
things happen
classic over achiever
strong and
smart while
I was
just trying
to make
everyone happy
except me
we looked
good on

paper
but in
our apartment
I was
a dead horse
and she was
a ghost rider
moving towards
the oblivion
that comes
after graduation.

Caretaking

Mark agreed
to watch
a professors
farm for
a year
while he
was away

he used
to carry
the chickens
by their feet
and he
pushed them
into my
face to
make me
nervous

he and
Eric sank
the professors
tractor in
the swamp
one night
after drinking

wine and
shooting
Eric's Gun

they survived
that winter
on fresh
eggs and
snow melted
on the stove
in order
to save
money to
pay for
the tractor

Eric liked
to tell
people
he lived
on a
farm but
Mark used
to say
this place
has 100
rooms but
none of

them are
worth
fucking
 or dying
 in.

Debie 2

Debie left
a year
ahead of me
she slept
with a
foreign guy
in Grad school
before she
went to
Africa and
spent nights
listening
to lions

it was
then she
realized that
her home town
and I
were things
she would
never see
again.

Billy

had been
driving and
trying to
cut lines
of coke
when his
car flipped
and he
ended up
in a
wheelchair

he lived
in an
assisted dorm
where student
workers helped
him shower
and dress
in time
for class

one night
coming home
drunk from
the bar

through snow
his chair
stalled
on the
path around
fake Lake

they found
him dead
the next day
frozen and
looking like
a snowman.

Brian

would walk
the humid
summer days
collecting
bones from
the fields
and farms
cow skulls
dog bones
bird wings
big pieces
tiny pieces
that he
would tie
together with
black thread

misshapen
puppets bleached
by summer
sun

we all
thought he
would go
study art

at the
local university
but he
said it
would ruin
the purity
of what
this is
and besides
the bones
tell me
how they
want to
come together
and no
professor
could teach
that

instead Brian
works for
Teds dad
all day
milking cows
and shoveling
manure

and spends

his nights
walking his
puppets through
his tiny
apartment

talking to
their bones.

The Hokker Brothers

competed at
everything
annoying everyone
around them
drunk one
time they
raced to
see who
could fill
a shot glass
with blood
from their
arms the
fastest and
they used
to joke
all the time
about playing
Russian Roulette

the summer
Jimmy drowned
down at
the Lake
George played
that game

with their
dads 22
pistol until
he lost.

Sara

was 18
when she
went to
have her
left breast
tattooed

the artist
got to
cup her boob
for better
than an
hour which
she knew
he loved

finishing the
outline he
said he
needed a
break and
she waited
20 minutes
before knocking
on the
bathroom door

she found him
dead with
a needle still
in his arm

a month later
when she
went
back to
have it
finished
everyone
remembered that
she called
the ambulance
and did CPR
so they
finished it
free and
promised
not to
leave the
room
this time

until it
was done.

Debbie's goodbye note

I called
off the
wedding then
she cheated
with the
English Grad
student and
I knew
we were
done when
I moved
the other
woman into
the apartment

one night
Debbie broke
in and
 hacked
the mattress
to shreds
with a
machete
stabbing a
note in
it that

said if
you think
your fucking
anyone else
in this
bed you're
wrong

this was
the first
time I
ever wondered
if she might
have loved
me after
all.

Tim

used to
get beat
by his
dad for
almost
any reason
bruises on
his back
and legs
a broken
wrist when
he was 10

at 16
Tim joined
the cross
country team
and ran
until his
lungs hurt
more than
his bruises
or scars

even though
he was

only the
fourth fastest
on the
team he
was happier
than we
had ever
seen him

on the
day his
dad died
from a
massive
heart attack
he ran
15 miles
without stopping

smiling
the whole
time.

Wanda

on the
day Wanda
hung herself
the ice
covered
the sidewalk
and her
car wouldn't
start she
was broke
hungry and
Zeke had
been dead
9 years
to the
day
so she
opened the
windows in
the hope
that the
cold would
keep the
smell down
until the
spring thaw

when maybe
someone
would find
her.

personal history

at the
end of
lonely roads
and old
farm houses
at the
end of
alcoholic fathers
and mothers
who never
move farther
than a few
miles from home
there's dying
land burned
fields reduced
to memories
of the lives
your grandparents
had
everybody drinks
and you take
what pills
you find
and the
local university

seems like
the only
way out

how you
graduate
and come
back home
is a sad
long story
you never
plan to
tell your
kids.

About the Author

Matthew Borczon is a nurse and Navy sailor from Erie, Pa. He has published four books of poetry, *A Clock of Human Bones* (Yellow Chair Review), *Battle Lines* (Epic Rites Press), *Ghost Train* (Weasel Publishing), *Sleepless Nights and Ghost Soldiers* (Grey Boarders), and *The Smallest Coffins are the Heaviest* (Epic Rites Punk Chapbook). He was a recipient of the Emerging Artist Grant in his hometown of Erie, Pa. He was nominated for a Pushcart and a Best of the Net for poetry in 2016. When not writing he raises four children with his wife of *21* years.

Nixes Mate Books features small-batch artisanal literature, created by writers that use all 26 letters of the alphabet and then some, honing their craft the time-honored way: one line at a time.

More Nixes Mate titles:
ON BROAD SOUND | Rusty Barnes
KINKY KEEPS THE HOUSE CLEAN | Mari Deweese
SQUALL LINE ON THE HORIZON | Pris Campbell
COMES TO THIS | Jeff Weddle
HITCHHIKING BEATITUDES | Michael McInnis
AIR & OTHER STORIES | Lauren Leja
WAITING FOR AN ANSWER | Heather Sullivan
A WORLD WHERE | Paul Brookes
MY SOUTHERN CHILDHOOD | Pris Campbell
THE PAUL BUNYAN BALLROOM | Bud Backen
THE WILLOW HOWL | Lisa Brognano

Forthcoming titles from Nixes Mate:
NIXES MATE REVIEW ANTHOLOGY 2016/17
LUBBOCK ELECTRIC | Anne Elezabeth Pluto
STARLAND | Jessica Purdy
SMOKEY OF THE MIGRAINES | Michael McInnis
JESUS IN THE GHOST ROOM | Rusty Barnes
HEART OF THE BROKEN WORLD | Jeff Weddle
SHE NEEDS THAT EDGE | Paul Brookes
HE WAS A GOOD FATHER | Mark Borczon

nixesmate.pub/books

www.ingramcontent.com/pod-product-compliance
Lightning Source LLC
Chambersburg PA
CBHW052135010526
44113CB00036B/2268